TITLE PAGE

We are the Vice Presidents of Employee Morale and Psychological Adjustment at the Corporate Coloring Co.

Follow the advice inside to color your way to the top of the business world, get paid for wasting time, and minimize stress levels by completely eliminating the need to do any real work.

This is my coloring book.

My name is:

....

My company is:

....

My title is:

....

My promoted title will be:

....

Written by Harriet Paul   Designed by Claire Munday   Images by Dooder/Shutterstock.com

Carry this on your person at all times during office hours, and follow the instructions on every page. Instructions are open to interpretation. The publisher cannot take responsibility for any job termination resulting from engagement with this book.

MATERIALS REQUIRED:
Coloring pens
Office supplies
Hands
Half a brain

OPTIONAL:
Other half of brain
Irritating coworkers
Increasingly bleak outlook
Personal boundaries
Sharp implements
Financial security
Matches
Lighter fluid
Midlife crisis
Coffee or tea
Tears

Get your thinking cap on!

In the event that you need disguise the book from seni management, turn swiftly the "safe" pages on pages 32-

COLOR YOURSELF IMPORTANT

First of all, you will need to dress for the job it appears you are doing. Color yourself as an executive.

COLORS YOU WILL NEED: Gray   Black

Briefcase Deface

Color this expensive briefcase and doodle the things you'll carry in it. Don't forget to add your initials in fancy lettering, so everyone knows it's yours.

Cubicle CULTURE

It is always best to avoid prolonged exposure to people in the office. Other people have the annoying habit of giving you work to do, or they simply have annoying habits. Find your way through the cubicle maze, avoiding the pests along the way.

START

Bad-tempered boss

The foghorn

O.M.G.

Office oversharer

Overenthusiastic intern

Overenthusiastic intern

Work-shy workmate

Backstabber

Overenthusiastic intern

FINISH

Daily Schedule

Busy and important people need a daily schedule so they can remember to do all of their busy and important things. Create your own:

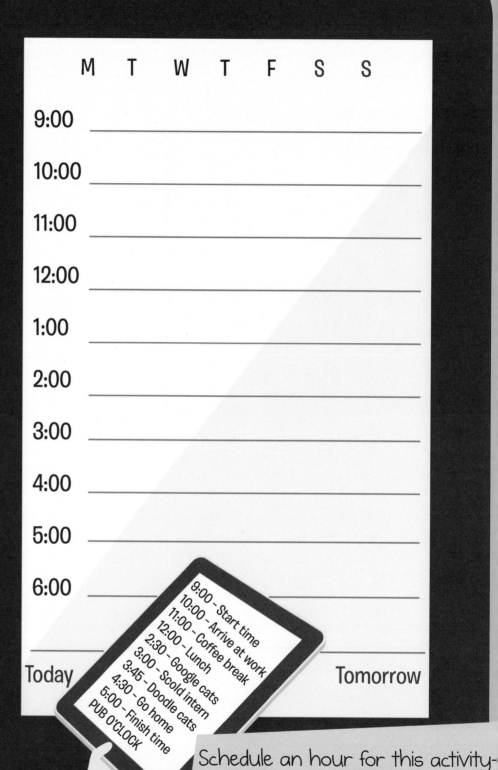

	M T W T F S S
9:00	
10:00	
11:00	
12:00	
1:00	
2:00	
3:00	
4:00	
5:00	
6:00	

Today   Tomorrow

9:00 – Start time
10:00 – Arrive at work
11:00 – Coffee break
12:00 – Lunch
2:30 – Google cats
3:00 – Scold intern
3:45 – Doodle cats
4:30 – Go home
5:00 – Finish time
PUB O'CLOCK

Schedule an hour for this activity- the boss won't mind. BEING ORGANIZED IS VERY IMPORTANT.

6

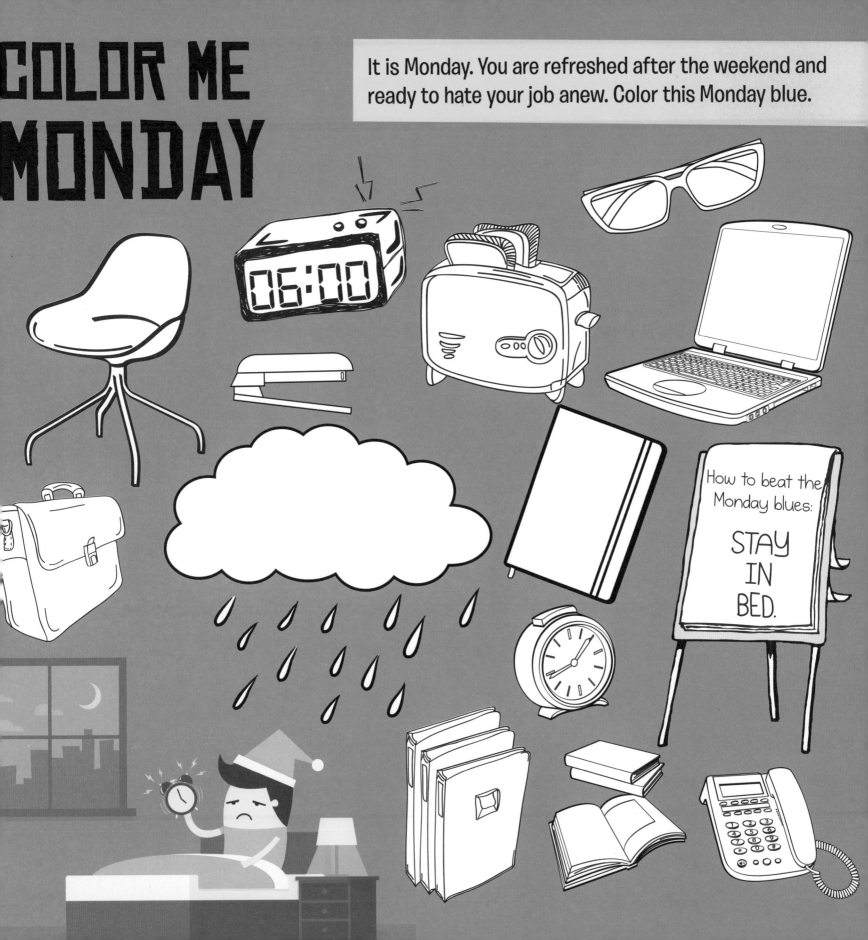

COLOR ME MONDAY

It is Monday. You are refreshed after the weekend and ready to hate your job anew. Color this Monday blue.

How to beat the Monday blues:

STAY
IN
BED.

Office DARES ✓

Start the day with ten push-ups in front of your desk. Count out loud.

For one day, sign off all emails with the words "nuff said."

When talking to a colleague, trail off your sentence, look vacant, and then suddenly announce, "So, it's a date!"

Type the following into a document and send it through to your boss's printer: "HELP ME, I'm stuck in the printer and I can't get out! Send for help!"

Kneel in front of the water cooler and drink directly from the nozzle.

Frame pictures of your "pets" and arrange them around your desk. The more obscure the pet the better (e.g. a blue whale, a flying squirrel, an ostrich).

During the course of a meeting, slowly edge your chair toward the door.

Burst into tears at the end of the day, claiming that you "don't want to go home."

Color
these ties snazzy.

Wearing a tie tells everyone that you are important. They will probably think that you are a banker, or maybe even a politician. Or, if you are not important, they let the important people know that you do not want to be fired.

Sweet tie.

Thanks, man.

Job Title Generator

It is essential you have a job title that is long, important-sounding, and just vague enough that nobody in the company can be quite sure what it is you do. This will ensure that you do not need to do much at all.

1. Pick one word from each column to create your NEW TITLE.

Corporate Coloring Co.

Vice President of Employee Morale and Psychological Adjustment

Ms. C. R. M. Jobsworth

Jobsworth@notathing.com
www.corporatecoloringdoesnotexist.com

2. Fill out BUSINESS CARDS (see press-outs) to give to your business associates.

You name it, YOU CLAIM IT!

Shiny new job title: ....

Your name: ....

Email address: ....

Draw your picture.

COLUMN 1	COLUMN 2	COLUMN 3
Bespoke	Operations Excellence	Architect
Differential	Information Configuration	Adviser
Senior	Virtual Enterprises	Consultant
Global	Disaster Recovery	Technician
Blue-Sky	Application Fulfillment	Developer
Core	Performance Solutions	Enabler
Internal	Infrastructure Mobility	Decision Maker
Lead	Business Decision	Integrator
Organic	Connectivity Tactics	Analyst
Online	Business Logistics	Specialist
Enterprising	Identity Implementation	Visionary
Executive	Marketing Metrics	Guru
Chief	Data Functionality	Overlord
Creative	Blog Integration	Captain
Expert	Hygiene Facilitation	Ninja
Direct	Information Enhancement	Strategizer
Corporate	Growth Security Directives	Commander
Dynamic	Inbound Communications	Champion
Heavyweight	Quality Assurance	Facilitator
International	Food Application Assembly	Associate
Principal	Human Branding	Officer
Entrepreneurial	World Changing	Agent
Strategic	Paradigm Optimization	Engineer
Future	Operations Configuration	Master
Head	Research Outsourcing	Director

COLOR A CUPPA

Coffee is a warm alternative to hating everybody, every morning, forever. Color a mug each time you have a cup of caffeinated goodness.

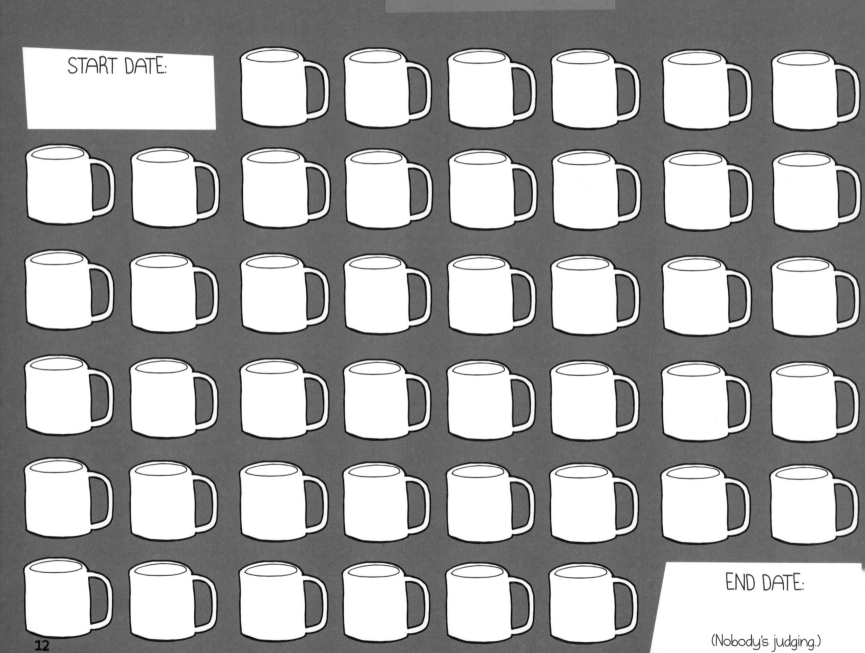

START DATE:

END DATE:

(Nobody's judging.)

NEVER answer your phone at work–that's what voicemail is for. People are usually only calling because they want YOU to do work for THEM, and that's just no way to behave.

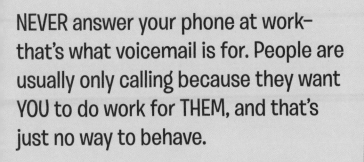

Write your voicemail message here:

CORPORATE Snakes & Career LADDERS

Fast-track your career and climb the corporate ladder in this tricky business board game. The first player to reach the top wins*!

*(nothing.)

YOU WILL NEED:

- 2-4 players
- Dice
- Character cards (see press-outs)
- Ruthless ambition

INSTRUCTIONS:

- Players should take turns rolling the dice and moving forward the correct number of spaces.
- Once they land on a space, players must perform any action mentioned.
- If a player lands on a space at the bottom of a ladder, they will climb the career path to the top of the ladder.
- Watch out for the office snakes—if a player lands on the head of a snake they must slide down to the bottom, thus being demoted to a lower position.
- The first player to reach the end of the board will WIN this crazy game they call business.

Dirty Doodling

Now you can create your very own office desk stain art, with extra whatthehellisthisonmydesk-iness! As they say, one worker's stain is another's work of art.

Dream Desk

Forget the dream job— the size of your desk is what it's really about. My desk is very large. It has many important things on it.

17

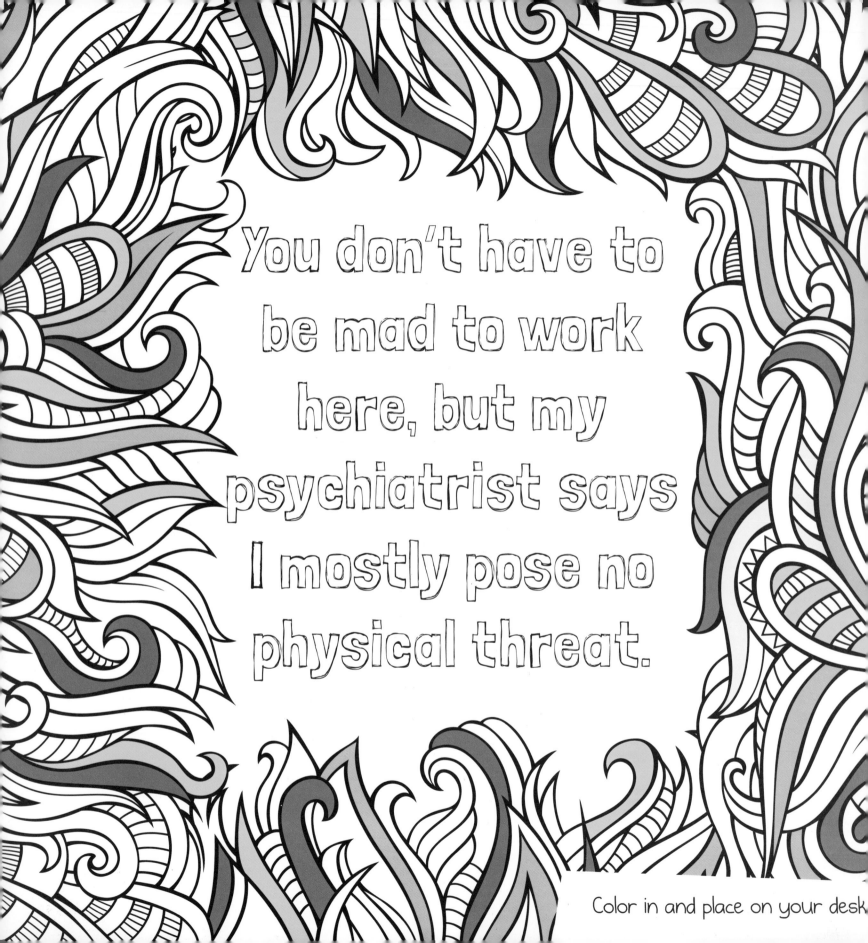

You don't have to be mad to work here, but my psychiatrist says I mostly pose no physical threat.

Color in and place on your desk

Color yourself calm.

JARGON BASEMENT

Keep this jargon dictionary handy to familiarize yourself with the latest office slanguage.

Al desco dining
Eating at your desk. Similar: Deskfast.

Blamestorming
A group meeting intended to assign responsibility for a failure.

Communicaking
A session where employers encourage staff to network by bribing them with baked goodness.

Decruiting
The politer way to fire someone.

Crapplicant
An applicant who is crap.

Fleemail
An email delegating responsibility while avoiding confrontation. Usually sent just before exiting the building.

Googlenosis
The act of looking up symptoms on the web to make your sickness more believable.

Headdesk
Unification of one's forehead with a desk in response to poor treatment or abject stupidity.

iTea department
A group of individuals who break up their day with excessive kettle boiling.

Ignoranus

A colleague who is both stupid and a dumbass.

McJob

A demeaning or low-ranking position.

OT mail

OverTime mail. The practice of sending your boss an unnecessary email, just to let them know how late you were working.

Mouse Potato

Someone who spends hour after hour sitting in front of a computer.

Notworking

A colleague who spends the day instant messaging people on company time.

Stroperator

The moody receptionist with an overinflated sense of importance.

Sledule

A schedule that continually slides due to poor planning and underestimated tasks.

T.W.A.T

A person who doesn't work Monday or Friday–only Tuesday, Wednesday, and Thursday.

Upskill

Skillful tweaking of a resume to improve one's experience and abilities, aka lying.

Vubicle

A cubicle next to a window = a cubicle with a view. Strategically allocated to help managers feel superior.

Workmare

A nightmare set in the workplace. Features extreme failure, hated coworkers, or horrible embarrassment.

Zombie project

A project that keeps coming back to life no matter how many attempts to kill it.

Tupper-where's the lid?!

Tupperware is useful for storing fresh food as well as leftover food you will never eat but will leave in the fridge until it goes moldy. Try to match these Tupperware boxes up with the right lids. *This* must be what they do at Tupperware parties!

Kindest of KIND REGARDS

Sometimes, we all wish "You dumbass" was an appropriate way to end a work email, but unfortunately, email etiquette dictates that it is not. Complete the word search for this and other insightful tips on how to send emails at work.

```
H T S E E A T T A C H E D P O I E
F P U L R G R E T T E L N I A H C
H I Y W S N N O P R O B L E M L M
N E T S V G R C D S W Q U H J B V
C C M P B N T X C A P S L O C K U
H E A M L O F R E T X D T R O H S
V R N D F W F I N M K R P K M N S
R D Y X F A H C T R E A A C G H A
C A T C F Y T F A I U G K E L M B
O E H C V F R D T N N E G H R T M
P R A G K T P O I U T R Z C S F U
I R N L L A Y L P E R D B L U G D
E D K L J L O V U I J N I L T G U
D R S F P H I R X C V I G E I L O
I Y N E R R H U I P L K U P C O Y
N Q R V U D O I T Y O U R S E L F
D E Q S X D E A R S I R S X H J U
```

GOOD WORDS:
REPLY
NO PROBLEM
DEAR SIR
SHORT
SPELLCHECK
MANY THANKS
SEE ATTACHED
COPIED
KIND REGARDS

BAD WORDS:
REPLY ALL
NO WAY
READ RECEIPT
CHAIN LETTER
CAPS LOCK
VIRUS
LOL
DO IT YOURSELF
YOU DUMBASS

23

OFFICE OLYMPICS ✦

Put the "abs" back into absence and capture the true spirit of teamwork by organizing an indoor office sporting event. It's time for the Interdepartmental Deskathlon!

YOU WILL NEED:

- Two or more teams
- An independent adjudicator to keep score

OPENING CEREMONY

Materials: paper, pencil, tape (to make your flag)

How to play: After making their own team flags, players from each team will take turns greeting the next person (a non-player) to walk through the office door, waving their team's flag. The independent adjudicator should rate each employee's greeting out of 10 based on style, enthusiasm, shock factor, and noise level. Team members may choose to forfeit their turn, but will earn no points.

WATER COOLER RELAY
TEAM EVENT

Materials: an approved area of track (e.g. the water cooler to one end of the office), a plastic cup

How to play: Players from each team should be spread out equally at pre-arranged points across the track. Starting at the water cooler with a full cup of water, the first player will run and pass the cup to the next player and so on, until the last person reaches the finish line. The team to finish first will receive 20 points, and the team to finish with the most water left in the cup at the end will receive 10 points.

PEN JAVELIN
TEAM EVENT

Materials: pens, name labels

How to play: Players from each team take turns to step up and hurl their pen as far they can from an approved starting point. The player who throws the farthest wins 20 points for their team. Players will be disqualified if their pen hits any humans but will receive 10 bonus points if any pen hits the boss.

✦ Please note that these Office Olympics are not affiliated with any real sporting event and participation in said events will not bring you any real fame or financial reward.

OFFICE CHAIR MARIO KART

2 PLAYERS

Materials: office chairs on wheels, an approved area of track, and obstacles to put in the track

How to play: One player sits on the office chair, while the second team member pushes them around the approved course, blindfolded. The player in the chair must shout out directions to guide them around the course. They must keep their arms folded at all times, their legs off the floor, and bum on the seat. The first team to cross the finish line is the winner! Award 30 points.

TRASH BIN BASKETBALL

2 PLAYERS

Materials: trash bins, basketballs (crushed paper)

How to play: Each player is to throw as many "basketballs" as they can into their opponent's trash bin, over one day. The opponent will try to defend their trash bin, though the bins cannot be moved. Competitors are encouraged to be sneaky and use as many diversionary tactics as they wish. For a valid goal, the thrower has to be at least 3 feet away. At the end of the day, whoever has the most balls in the other competitor's trash bin is the winner, and will be awarded 30 points.

SACK RACE

1 PLAYER

Materials: termination form, pen

How to play: One member from each team will be nominated to complete a job termination form. The winner is the participant to complete the form in the quickest time, earning 20 points for their team. All fields must be completed and a 5-second penalty will be added to the overall time for each incorrect or missing field.

CLOSING CEREMONY

Congratulations, you have successfully completed your first Office Olympics! Winning team members should be presented with a medal, using the press-outs at the back of the book, and interlinked paperclips. They can then take the entire afternoon off for their show of team spirit, enthusiasm, and commitment to office morale. The losing teams will make the coffee for 1 week.

This is your boss's ass. Color it in. Practice kissing it.

Kiss ass.

The Office PRINTER

This is not just any printer. It is a mediocre printer, a mediocre scanner, AND a mediocre copier! With a special bonus feature–it crunches up your paper, free of charge!

Turn this brand-spanking-new printer into the PAPER-EATING MONSTER it will inevitably turn out to be.

Excuses, Excuses

This flow chart will help you answer the age-old question we adults face on a daily basis: Should I call in sick today?

START

Are you meant to be at work today?

NO →

Congratulations! You had the foresight to book time off in advance. Enjoy your holiday.

YES →

Do you want to go to work today?

NO →

Are you actually sick?

NO. But I am sick of going to wo

YES *cough cough*→

Aww, poor you. Better get your best sick voice ready...

EXCUSES!

YES →

Seriously? Yeah right. Are you lying to me and to yourself?

NO →

Then what are you reading this quiz for, loser? Get to work!

YES. PSYCH! →

Go back to the start and tell the truth this time.

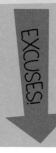

"I'M SORRY I CAN'T COME TO WORK TODAY BECAUSE..."
Proceed to explain your genuine reason and go to the doctor/hospital if necessary.
UNLESS!
You are dying. In this case, hang up the phone immediately and never go to work again.

Will you get fired if you don't go in?

— YES → **Do you care if you are fired?** — NAH → **Work sucks.**

— It's a possibility → **Do you care if you are fired?**

— NO → **My being away will give everyone else a chance to shine.**

Do you care if you are fired? — YES → **I need my job to live/pay my bills/be a responsible adult.**

Work sucks. — EXCUSES! →

My being away will give everyone else a chance to shine. — EXCUSES! →

"I'M SORRY I CAN'T COME TO WORK TODAY. I HAVE…"

"Food poisoning." Go into graphic detail for best results.

"Women's problems." If you are male, you may delete the "s" from "women's."

"Head lice." No one will want you to come anywhere near them.

"A 12/24/48-hour stomach bug." Choose whichever time frame suits best.

"A pet emergency." No one can argue with a cute animal in trouble.

I need my job to live/pay my bills/be a responsible adult. → Go to work, quick! → **Are you late now after reading this pointless quiz?**

Are you late now after reading this pointless quiz?

— YES → "I'M SORRY I AM LATE. I…"

— NO → **Great! Enjoy your soul-destroying day in the office!**

"I'M SORRY I AM LATE. I…"

"Have children." An excellent excuse for most things—just blame it on those snotty little brats.

"Locked myself out naked and had to wait for a locksmith." Also works for car keys (minus the nakedness).

"Was the only witness to a crime." Any crime will do.

"Forgot to feed the hamster."

"I CAN'T COME TO WORK TODAY 'CAUSE…"

"I have band practice."

"My goldfish needed a holiday."

"My bed needs me. We're kind of going through a rough patch."

"I didn't forward a chain email to 20 people yesterday."

"I have to get drunk to forget how much I hate my job."

"The top I want to wear is dirty."

"It's raining."

"I thought dress down Friday meant stay in your PJs all day… at home."

Great! Enjoy your soul-destroying day in the office!

Office Crush

It is a good idea to cultivate an office crush to pass the time at work. You can stare at them in meetings, daydream about holding hands, draw them when they're not looking...

This is my office crush. Her name is Melanie.

My office crush is called:

Water Cooler Chat

Ah, the water cooler, the traditional office meeting place for many a thirsty slacker. Find a friend on the search for your next sip by making use of these excellent water cooler ice-breakers.

Did you watch Game of Thrones last night?

Do you like coffee? 'Cause I like you a latte.

Have you seen what the boss is wearing today?

Did you see the latest Bond movie? (Because there will always BE a Bond movie.)

Are you having lunch al desco today?

What are you doing at month end?

How about that game last night?

Oh hey, I drew this really cool picture of you. It's in my drawer. Would you like to come and see it?

No?

Latest Company S.T.A.T.S.*

This is your safe page—keep it bookmarked so that if your boss or a goody-two-shoes colleague walks past and catches you mid–inappropriate activity, you can quickly flip to this page. It's full of realistic-looking graphs and boring text and stuff. This will ensure you keep your job while still avoiding doing any work. Resume your activity once the coast is clear.

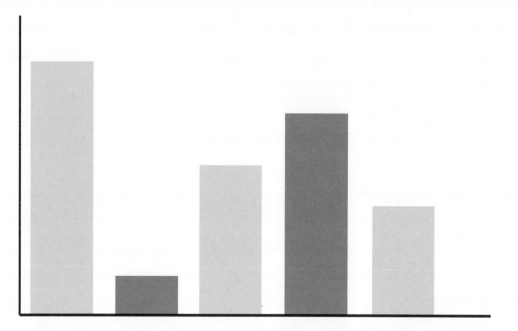

Things at your company are looking really, really good at the moment. Probably. I mean, I have no idea really—if you're coloring in this book at work it's probably bloody awful. However, if you look at the graph above, you will see that there are more green bars than red, and everyone knows that green is generally a better color than red. (These are some things that are good that are green: grass, leaves, avocados, money. Things that are good that are red: not a lot.) Speaking of money, can you believe that you're getting paid right now to read this rubbish? Incredible. Well done, you. It's probably best to highlight a couple of sentences right now just to make sure

it looks like you're doing something. Making notes in the columns is also a good trick. Hell, just underline some random words.

Numbered points make things look important:

1. 4.4 million employees now spend their time coloring at work.
2. Profits are higher than ever, claims a report. Bonuses are surely guaranteed.
3. Further research suggests that the workforce is more productive if fed a pie on the hour, every hour. See opposite page for an in-depth pie analysis.
4. Science says that workforces will work faster if spoon-fed cake from 9 a.m. to 5 p.m. (source unverified).

*Something To Avoid The Sack.

Employee of the Decade

Breaking news: A cartoon character has been awarded the coveted title of Employee of the Decade at a nonexistent event, in an undisclosed area last night. Scandal broke out when the losing nominees started a violent brawl after the winner was announced. No participants were available for comment, but we did speak to a member of the audience who said it was "insane. Absolutely freaking insane." In other coverage, we can announce that several of the women at the awards wore dresses and shoes, and some had clutch bags, too. Turn to page 89 for a full run-through of all the hot outfits and the not outfits.

Profits are Really High

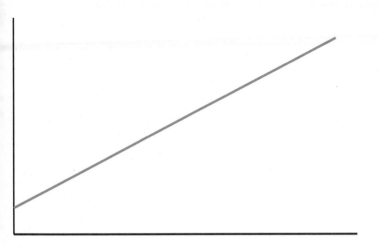

This is very unlikely considering the amount of work that you are currently doing. What this graph actually shows is the correlation between productivity and caffeine intake. This would suggest you should spend 2 hours a day making coffee to maximize output. It's cold, hard science. While you're at it, get some cake. Graphs pointing upward suggest that eating cake is directly correlated to breathing.

NEWS: Workforce Best in Country

This headline makes little to no sense. It's easy to make no sense while still sounding like you could be making sense, by speaking business-speak. Just string unconnected jargon words together in a sentence to impress and confuse your colleagues. The bottom line is, employers need to display more transparency when disclosing profit margins and strategy ideation to key stakeholders, heretofore. The output is not monetized per se, therefore it is evident that they must sense check solutions before they can deliver the deliverables. Best practice indicates that solutioning is related to the high headcount and the low-hanging fruit. Consequently, if staff can capture synergies with hyper collaboration initiatives and reach out and touch base, the world would be a better place.

A Sweet Pie Chart

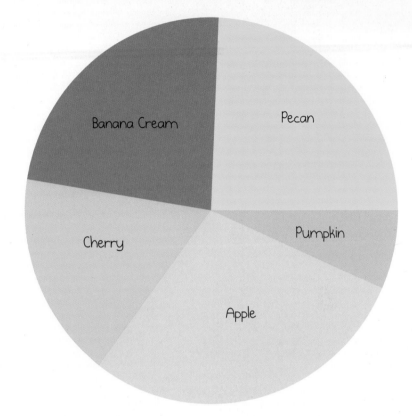

I like pies. Who doesn't like pies? There are all sorts of different pies that didn't make this sweet pie chart, because a) they didn't all fit, and b) they weren't all sweet. Such as: Blueberry pie. Peach pie. Lemon meringue pie. Key lime pie. Gooseberry pie. Rhubarb pie. Raspberry pie. Mississippi mud pie. Blackberry pie. Mince pie. Steak and ale pie. Chicken pie. Meat and potato pie.

Pork pie. Cottage pie. Shepherd's pie. Steak and kidney pie. Sweet potato pie. Fish pie. There are also all sorts of different pie charts you could make about pies. Your favorite types of pie: sweet pies, savory pies, summer pies, autumn pies, winter pies. The best things about pies. The best pie accompaniments. Favorite pastry for pies. Places they serve pies. You get the idea.

Boardroom LINGO BINGO

Here are some key words for pretending you know a lot about everything at work. Memorize them and use them freely in conversations with corporate types. Or laugh at other people using them to liven up a boring meeting.

IDEATION	SOLUTIONING	GOING FORWARD	HIT THE GROUND RUNNING	STAKEHOLDERS
TRANSPARENT	TOUCH BASE	TEACHABLE MOMENT	PROFIT MARGIN	THE BOTTOM LINE
QUICK QUESTION	REACH OUT	IN THE PIPELINE	IMPLEMENT	OUTSOURCE
NO-BRAINER	BEST PRACTICE	LEVERAGE	ON MY RADAR	BENCHMARK
PUT YOUR THINKING CAP ON	FAST TRACK	REVISIT	MONETIZING	PER SE

Challenge a colleague to a game of boardroom lingo bingo!
RULES: Photocopy these pages. Each player should take a bingo card and a beverage of their choice into the meeting. Color a box every time a word is used, as well as taking a sip of your drink each time. The first person to fill a row of five words is the lingo bingo champion! Loser: Down your drink! (Note: Yelling "BINGO!" is optional, but advised.)

THINK OUTSIDE THE BOX	BALLPARK	EQUITY	WORKSHOP	INTERFACE
TAKE IT OFFLINE	SYNERGY	ACTION ITEMS	HEADS-UP	REINVENT THE WHEEL
SENSE CHECK	COOPERATE	BLUE-SKY THINKING	DOWNSIDE	STRATEGY
HEADCOUNT	B TO B	ON THE SAME PAGE	OUT OF THE LOOP	LOW-HANGING FRUIT
DELIVERABLES	BRAINSTORM	BUSINESS-WISE	FACILITATE	YIELD

No office fridge is complete without a hostile standoff over a stolen sandwich. Add your own passive-aggressive (or plain aggressive-aggressive) notes to the fridge to kick off kitchen warfare.

Hi everybody, I am the fridge and I have had ENOUGH.

Please put new food in the fridge. Getting bored of the same old stuff.

I don't know who you are, but you have been stealing my sauce. Put it back in the fridge or I will LICK EVERYTHING.

Label the food items, color in, and add a
layer of mold to the leftovers.

Nothing in
this lunch
box is worth
dying for.

I sneezed
in this
sandwich.

Highlight
of the Day

PLAYER 1

START

FINISH

Challenge a colleague to a highlighter pen showdown. The first one to the finish line (keeping a neatly highlighted line) will be named the Ultimate Office Tool Champion!

PLAYER 2

START

FINISH

Let It Tea

MUG

Nothing can ruin your day quite like a poorly made cup of tea or coffee. Get coworkers to sign up under their ideal blend, then give this page to the office intern to ensure a perfect cup, every time.

Skimmed alive	Weakly committed	Strip-teas	Bland blend	Long Island	Iron brew
Milky way	Pale & boring	Cha cha cha	Two week tan	Golden oldie	Builder's brew
Dishwater delight	Earl gravy	Cuppa cabana	Hip-stir	Burnt toast	Ink black

If your preference isn't here, color and create your own!

WARNING: Under NO circumstances should you put the milk in the mug first.

Cookie Mountain

Keep calm

Dull Desk Coloring

What better way is there to ~~waste~~ spend your time at work than coloring in an assortment of office objects?

Color this page using only office supplies, then label every item with your name.

Without STUPID PEOPLE we would have no one to laugh at.

Take time out to thank a stupid person for their contribution to the office.

Color this page in. Tear it out and turn over for instructions on how to make it into a paper airplane. Proceed to send your THANKS across the office.

Many thanks.

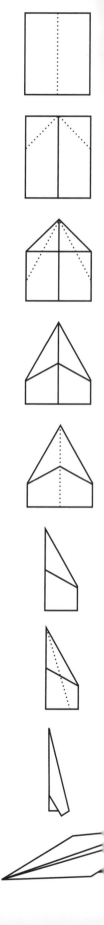

DREAM VIEW

Attempt to brighten up your life and your surroundings by doodling the view you wish you could see out of your office window.

Office DARES ✓

For one day, whenever you speak, hold your pen to your mouth like a microphone.

While riding in the elevator, gasp dramatically every time the doors open.

Go to the bathroom and change into swimwear. Splash tap water all over yourself. Return to your desk saying, "It's lovely by the pool."

At the end of a meeting, stay behind as everyone else, including the person who called the meeting, leaves. Thank each person for coming.

Put a sign on an empty glass meeting room saying "Invisibility Seminar—All Day."

During a meeting, wink at someone at the table. Slowly work your way around the table, winking at everyone. Sometimes shake your head just a little, as if to indicate that the speaker is slightly crazy and everybody knows it.

Speed up a colleague's mouse so it is uncontrollable. Tell them they need to cut back on the caffeine and/or imply that they have a drug problem.

Whenever anyone gives you something to do, ask if they "want fries with that?"

Color a Colleague

Draw and color the coworker sitting next to you. Stick the drawing up at your desk when you're finished. Leave it there until they ask you to take it down.

Colleague of the Week

Sometimes, the best thing about my job is that the chair swivels.

Color these chairs to take your mind off the fact you'll probably still be sitting in yours when you're 60.

50

TIPS TO GET TO THE TOP
(WITHOUT EVEN TRYING)

1. Walk quickly wherever you go. This will create the impression you are busy doing things, so people will be less likely to stop you and give you anything else to do.

2. Always walk with a document in your hands. People with documents in their hands look like hardworking employees heading for important meetings, even when they are lazy employees heading to the cafeteria.

3. Use technology to look busy. Any time you use a computer or a laptop it looks like "work" to the casual observer. You can send personal emails, chat, and have a blast without doing anything remotely related to work.

4. Be mediocre. Being great at your job simply means your lazy colleagues will bring their unwanted work directly to you. Always complete your work just adequately enough to avoid being fired.

ANGER MANAGEMENT

Save this activity for a really, really bad day, and take out your pent-up anger on the page instead of unsuspecting coworkers. No jail, yay!

Draw a picture pushing **REALLY HARD** with the pencil.

Chuck sharp pencils at the dartboard.

Scribble violently.

Poke holes in the page.

Tear, bite, or scratch the page using a sharp object.

TEARS go here.

53

Safe or Dangerous?

Are these office objects 100 percent harmless or a Health and Safety nightmare? You decide! Doodle up some office dream or deathtrap scenarios involving these innocuous-looking items.

OUTFIT ORIGAMI

Now you can turn your useless notes into even more useless 3D clothes!

TO MAKE THE TIE: You'll need a sticky note.

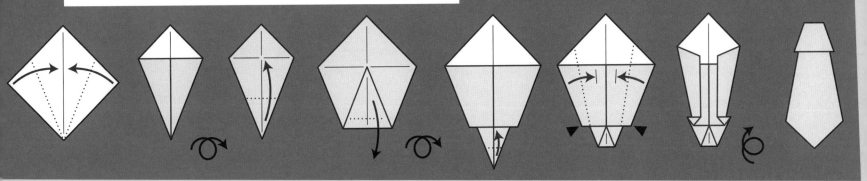

TO MAKE THE SHIRT: You'll need a piece of letter paper.

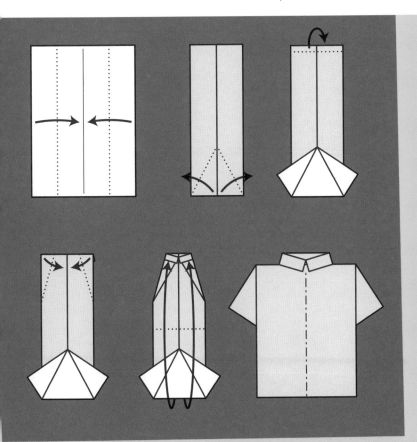

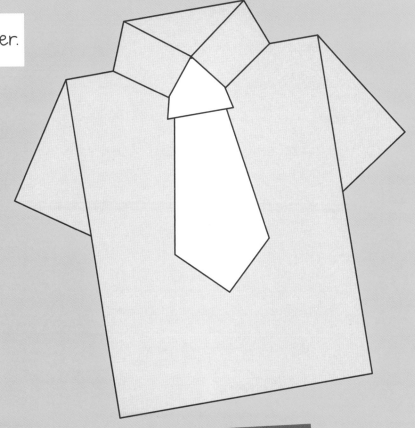

Now draw, color, and doodle all over your new outfit.

PASSIVE-AGGRESSIVE NOTES

A POEM FOR A PILFERER
Just 'cause my sandwich had no name
did not mean it was fair game.
I did not prepare it and waste my time for it
to end up in YOUR mouth and not in MINE.
In short, I hope you choke on it
you stupid, little thieving _____.

No, I did not watch Game of Thrones last night. Please stop talking about it!!

Do not use whimsical fonts.

Do NOT unplug the coffee maker.

I have received complaints about too many notes being placed here. Please stop putting up notes, guys!!!

UNI-COLLEAGUE

Convert your work calamities to calmness by transforming your colleagues into colorful unicorns! Go the extra mile and give them crazy manes and ridiculous names.

LARRY FROM ACCOUNTS =
Princey Rainbow
Nostrils

Happiness is...

clocking out of work for the day and heading home.

DIY Catapult

Looking for something fun to do with all those office supplies you've been "collecting" from work? Make the necessary preparations for inter-desk conflict with this DIY office catapult.

YOU WILL NEED:
- A large binder clip
- Strong tape
- A pen or a pencil
- Rubber band

1. Hold the binder clip in an upsidedown triangle, lay one handle flat on the desk and tape the middle of it down to the desk.

2. Fold the binder clip's body down over the taped handle. Hold the clip down and set a pencil on top of the exposed side of the clip.

3. Keeping the pencil in place, wrap a rubber band over the two handles, twisting the band at the end and wrapping it over again until tight.

4. Now ball up your strip of paper. Hold the bottom handle while you place your ammo on the top handle, pull back the lever, and FIRE!

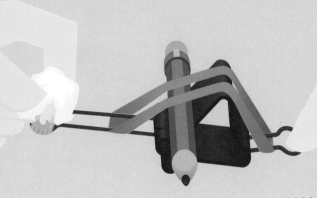

TEAR AND CRUMPLE TO MAKE YOUR AMMO

Correction Coloring

Cover up your troubles and create a picture using only white-out pen on these pages.

Stick the staple in the boss.

Challenge an office ally to a round of "stick it to the boss" stapler bull's-eye for some manager-related sharp relief.

Use a tie as a blindfold!

50 40 30 20 10

ALTERNATIVE AMMO:
- Thumb tacks
- Sharpened pencils
- Ink cartridges

PARTY Time!

Are you overworked and underintoxicated? Never fear, the office party is here! Whether it's the Christmas shindig or the summer social, color and complete this guide post-session to piece together what went down.

Told inappropriate jokes to coworkers.

Color how many drinks were drunk.

Misused the photocopier. Oh God, where did you leave the copies?!

You can't drink at work!

Don't worry, I'm not working.

Told your office crush you have a crush on them.

Urgh...

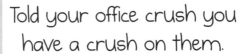

Told your boss to go ✸✸✸✸ themself.
Probably don't bother going into work today.

Turn to page 28 for a suitable excuse if you woke up too hungover/embarrassed to show your face at work.

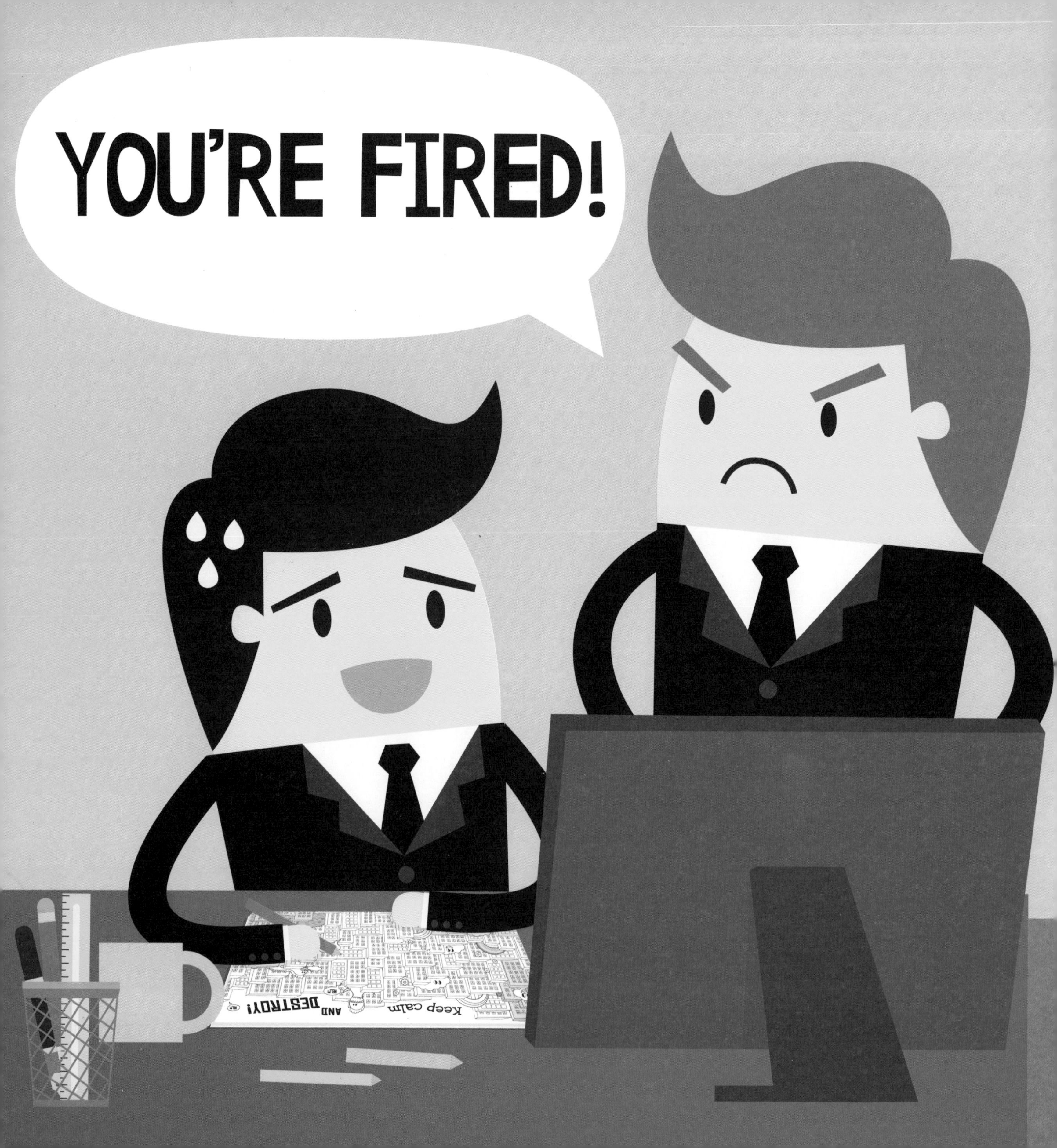
YOU'RE FIRED!
Keep calm AND DESTROY!